anythin

THE UNITED STATES PRESIDENTS

WILLIAM HOWARD

TAFT

OUR 27TH PRESIDENT

by Melissa Maupin

The Child's World®
childsworld.com

1980 Lookout Drive • Mankato, MN 56003-1705
800-599-READ • www.childsworld.com

ACKNOWLEDGMENTS
Content Adviser: David R. Smith, Adjunct Assistant
Professor of History, University of Michigan–Ann Arbor

PHOTOS
Cover and page 3: North Wind Picture Archives
Interior: Associated Press, 11; Chronicle/Alamy Stock Photo, 14;
Circa Images/Newscom, 18, 23, 32; Everett Collection/Newscom,
21; Everett Historical/Shutterstock.com, 26, 36, 39 (bottom right);
George W. Harris/Newscom, 17; Library of Congress, Prints and
Photographs Division, 7, 8, 9, 12, 15, 16, 20, 22, 25, 27, 30, 31,
34, 35, 38 (right), 39 (left and top right); North Wind Picture
Archives, 4, 10, 28, 38 (left); Picture History/Newscom, 33;
Picture History/Newscom, 6; US National Park Service, 5, 24

ISBN 9781503844186 (REINFORCED LIBRARY BINDING)
ISBN 9781503847224 (PORTABLE DOCUMENT FORMAT)
ISBN 9781503848412 (ONLINE MULTI-USER EBOOK)
LCCN 2019957766

Printed in the United States of America

CONTENTS

*William Howard Taft
served as president
from 1909 to 1913.*

A LEGACY OF LAW

William Howard Taft grew up surrounded by discussions of law and **politics.** His father, Alphonso Taft, served as a judge and then the secretary of war under President Ulysses S. Grant. William loved hearing about his father's travels and trials. He dreamed of following a similar path in life. He was especially interested in becoming a judge. This was

his lifelong goal, and one day he would achieve it—and more. By the end of his career, William Taft had become the only man in American history to serve as both president and chief justice of the Supreme Court.

William Taft was born in Cincinnati, Ohio, on September 15, 1857. He was a healthy, happy child who laughed easily. Taft's parents, Louisa and Alphonso, believed strongly in education. They pushed William to study and make good grades. He was a bright and eager student.

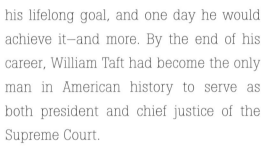

William Howard Taft was the only person ever to serve as president and chief justice of the United States.

William Taft was born into a prominent Ohio family. He grew up in Cincinnati in this grand house. In this photograph from around 1868, a young William is standing at the fence, and his brother Henry is seated on the post.

Taft attended Yale University in Connecticut, just as his father and two older half-brothers had. Yale was among the best colleges in the country. Taft was popular with the other students, who enjoyed his good nature and sense of humor. They nicknamed him "Big Bill" because, by then, Taft stood six feet two inches (188 cm) tall and was stocky in build.

William suffered a serious accident when he was nine years old. He was riding in a horse-drawn carriage when the horse was startled and took off running. The carriage was wrecked, and William was dragged along, his head bumping on the ground. He nearly died from the accident and had to have many stitches on his head, leaving a large scar.

In 1878, Taft graduated second in his class at Yale University and enrolled at Cincinnati Law School. Taft finished law school in 1880 and became licensed to practice law. Instead of working at a law firm, Taft landed a job working as a court reporter for a Cincinnati newspaper, the *Commercial Gazette*.

This was the last job for which he would ever apply. From that time forward, he was **appointed** to a variety of jobs in the government. People liked Taft's skill, intellect, and friendly style. He accepted his first appointment just one year out of law school. He left his job as court reporter to become the assistant **prosecutor** of Hamilton County. Then, in 1882, President Chester Arthur appointed him the tax collector for the Cincinnati area. He was the youngest tax collector in the country at that time.

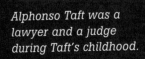

Alphonso Taft was a lawyer and a judge during Taft's childhood.

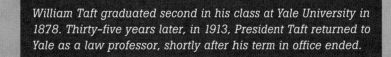

At age 29, Taft was named to the Ohio State Superior Court. He was thrilled with this opportunity because, more than anything, Taft wanted to be a judge. At this point in his career, he already had begun to dream of sitting on the most powerful court in the country, the United States Supreme Court.

During his early career, Taft fell in love with Helen Herron, whom he called Nellie. Taft visited Nellie at her home, where young men and women gathered and talked about popular books they had read. Like Taft's mother, Nellie was an intelligent, well-educated woman from a respected family.

Taft's father discouraged him from participating in too many sports. He wanted his son to concentrate on making good grades. Later, as president, Taft learned to love sports, especially golf. Americans saw how much Taft liked the sport and began trying golf for themselves. The number of golfers on public golf courses doubled while Taft was president.

Nellie was cool to Taft at first, and he worried that she would never marry him. Finally, she made him a happy man by accepting his proposal of marriage. They wed on June 19, 1886, and later had three children: Charles, Helen, and Robert. The Tafts' marriage was the beginning of a strong partnership. Nellie's opinions and her faith in her husband's abilities would play an important role in his future.

THE TAFTS OF CINCINNATI

William Taft is the most famous person in his family, but Cincinnati's Taft family has a long tradition of education and success. Taft's great-grandfather Aaron Taft worked as a town clerk. His grandfather Peter was a judge, a justice of the peace, and a member of the Vermont state legislature, the lawmaking body for that state. Taft's father, Alphonso, felt strongly that any government appointment was an honor. Alphonso was a judge and served as the secretary of war, just as his son would one day.

Taft's older half-brothers, Charles and Peter, both graduated from Yale and practiced law. Charles later became a US congressman. Taft's younger brothers, Henry and Horace, both graduated from Yale, too. Henry went on to practice law, and Horace opened a school for boys.

The tradition continued with later generations. Both of William Taft's sons became lawyers. His older son, Robert (pictured below in 1939), became a leading US senator. His younger son, Charles, was elected the mayor of Cincinnati. Taft's grandson, Robert Jr., also became a US senator. His great-grandson, Robert III, was elected governor of Ohio in 1999.

CLIMBING THE POLITICAL LADDER

At age 32, William Taft felt he might have a chance to achieve his goal to become a judge on the highest court of the country. He found out that President Benjamin Harrison might choose him to be justice on the US Supreme Court. He knew that this was a long shot, because he was probably too young and inexperienced for such an important position. Taft joked that his chances of winning the job were about equal to his chances

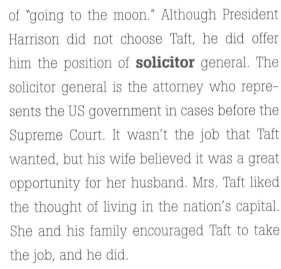

of "going to the moon." Although President Harrison did not choose Taft, he did offer him the position of **solicitor** general. The solicitor general is the attorney who represents the US government in cases before the Supreme Court. It wasn't the job that Taft wanted, but his wife believed it was a great opportunity for her husband. Mrs. Taft liked the thought of living in the nation's capital. She and his family encouraged Taft to take the job, and he did.

Taft became a judge on the US Circuit Court when he was just 34 years old.

Nellie Taft had high hopes for her husband. He wanted to be a judge, but she wanted him to be president.

Two years later, 34-year-old Taft heard that a position was opening on the United States Circuit Court. This was one of the highest courts in the country. Taft wanted the job, and to his delight, it was offered to him. He moved his family from Washington back to Cincinnati and began traveling to various cities to hear trials. Nellie was not as pleased with the change as her husband was. She felt that Taft should stay in Washington, DC, where he could meet the most powerful people in politics. Taft did not care for political life, however. He felt more comfortable in the courtroom dealing with the law.

A young girl works at a cotton mill in Georgia. In the late 1800s, many people began trying to end child labor. They argued that many children's jobs were dangerous. Also, if children worked long hours, they could not go to school.

Taft served on the circuit court from 1892 until 1900. In this position, he ruled on many issues involving the workplace. At the time, many American workers were not paid fairly for their work. Some worked in crowded, unhealthy, and dangerous places. Children also commonly worked in factories. Many of them did not go to school. They worked long hours and performed dangerous jobs, just like the adults in the factory.

Unhappy workers began to band together to form **labor unions.** The unions demanded fair working conditions and pay. Some unions went on **strike.** The union members refused to work until they got what they wanted. Business owners grew angry and refused to give in to the employees. Both unions and businesses sometimes used violence when they did not get their way.

As a judge, Taft made enemies with some leaders of the labor unions. He believed the workers deserved better treatment, but he also believed that the labor unions had to obey the law. If Taft felt they had broken the law, he ruled against them.

One day in 1900, Taft received a message from President William McKinley offering him a surprising challenge. The United States had just finished fighting the Spanish-American War. In the **treaty** that ended the war, Spain gave the United States control of the Philippines, a group of islands located in the Pacific Ocean southeast of Asia. President McKinley was sending a **commission** to take control of the islands. He asked Taft to serve as the commission president.

Taft did not feel qualified for this position. Again, Nellie and his family encouraged him to accept the job. The US secretary of war, Elihu Root, also urged him to take the job. Finally, Taft decided to try his hand at governing the islands.

When Taft reached the Philippines, he realized what a difficult job lay ahead of him. The country was made up of more than 7,000 islands, and the people spoke seven different languages. Most of them lived in poor conditions, there were no schools, and outbreaks of violence were common.

Nellie Taft first visited the White House when she was just 17 years old. Her family was there to see her father's friend, President Rutherford B. Hayes. Afterward, she announced that she liked the president's mansion so much, she planned to marry a man who would one day become president.

Taft traveled on horseback throughout the Philippines, getting to know the people. Soon they grew to trust him. In 1901, Taft became the official governor of the islands. He enjoyed working with the Filipino people. He created a plan to help them set up their own government. His first steps were to construct a good road system and to organize local governments. Next, he worked to set up schools, courts, and basic services for the people.

Taft arrived in the Philippines in 1900. In this picture, houseboats line a river in Manila, the capital city of the Philippines.

William Taft (pictured in his office in the Philippines) enjoyed his time working with the Filipino people. As governor of the Philippines, Taft helped to establish the government and laws, as well as perform many civil services, including building new roads, schools, and health care facilities.

Life in the Philippines could be uncomfortable. The climate was hot and steamy. Violent tropical storms sometimes blew across the islands. There were also many mosquitoes. During his time in the Philippines, Taft suffered from severe stomach problems and other difficulties that made him ill. Even with these health problems, he weighed close to 300 pounds (136 kg). The extra weight made the trips across the islands on horseback even more uncomfortable.

Taft believed in equality for all people. He hated how white people treated black people. He tried to find positions for blacks in the government but found it difficult. "The prejudice against them is so strong that it makes few places available," he wrote to his wife, "and yet I must do something for the race, for they are entitled to recognition."

THE TAFT FAMILY IN
THE PHILIPPINES

When Taft left for the Philippines in 1900, he took his family with him. This photograph shows the Tafts and other members of President McKinley's commission as they make their way to the islands southeast of Asia. William Taft (second from right) plays a card game with his wife, Nellie, and two others.

Mrs. Taft was especially excited about the chance to travel so far from home. She read everything she could find about the Philippines. The family sailed to Hawaii and then Japan. Finally, they arrived in the Philippine city of Manila, where they would live for the next four years.

The time spent in the Philippines was mostly happy for the Tafts. They had a cook and several servants, yet their day-to-day life was simple. Mrs. Taft traveled with her husband all around the islands.

The children made friends and attended school. They rode ponies and kept a monkey, an orangutan, and a deer as pets. They also learned to speak the local language.

CHAPTER THREE

PRESSURED INTO THE PRESIDENCY

While Taft was enjoying his work in the Philippines, something tragic happened in the United States. In September 1901, Taft learned that President McKinley had been murdered. Taft was saddened and shaken by this news. He had respected the president, and McKinley had supported his work in the Philippines. Taft wondered what the future would hold for him, his job, and his country with a new president.

Vice President Theodore Roosevelt became president following McKinley's death. Taft was unsure what Roosevelt thought about his job in the Philippines. He was relieved to learn that Roosevelt admired his work.

In fact, when a position opened on the Supreme Court, Roosevelt offered Taft the seat. Surprisingly, Taft turned him down, even though he had long dreamed of being a Supreme Court justice. He felt that he should finish his work in the Philippines first.

Although he was a warm and kind man, William Taft was not a strong leader.

As secretary of war, Taft supervised the building of the Panama Canal. As president, he returned to Panama to tour the construction site. In this picture, President Taft (center, in white suit) views the canal's construction in 1910.

When Roosevelt was elected for his second term as president, he asked Taft to become a member of his **cabinet** as the secretary of war. This opportunity came at a good time for Taft. His work in the Philippines was nearly finished. He had also grown quite ill. He needed to return to the United States to recover.

Because he was likable and had a strong sense of fairness, Taft was an excellent secretary of war. He managed to calm leaders and rebels in Cuba following a **revolution.** He also helped write a treaty between Japan and Russia following the Russo-Japanese War. Then, Roosevelt sent him to Panama to oversee the building of the Panama Canal.

This 50-mile-long (80-km) canal would cut across the narrowest part of Central America, creating a short route from the Atlantic to the Pacific ocean. Ships would no longer have to travel all the way around the tip of South America to get from one ocean to the other.

By 1908, Roosevelt's presidency was coming to an end. Many members of the Republican Party thought Taft should run for president. At age 51, he had decades of experience in many different government jobs. Yet Taft shied away from the presidency. He still pictured himself as a judge, not as a politician. Taft wanted Roosevelt or Elihu Root to run, but neither man would. They both urged Taft to run for the Republican Party **nomination.**

Nellie had longed for many years to see her husband become president. She and his brothers pushed him to run for the nomination. Only Taft's mother recognized the true nature of her son. "I do not want my son to be president," she said. "His is a judicial mind and he loves the law."

As secretary of war, Taft traveled more than any other cabinet minister. He spent more than 255 days working in foreign countries.

Taft usually took Nellie and one or two of his children on his trips as secretary of war. His travels cost the government a good deal of money. Finally, President Roosevelt asked Taft to have his brother Charles help pay for the trips. Charles Taft was wealthy and agreed to help fund his brother's travels.

President Theodore Roosevelt's support helped Taft win the presidency in 1908. This illustration shows Roosevelt as a king holding Taft, the prince who would take over the throne.

Soon it became clear that William Jennings Bryan would likely be the Democratic Party's **candidate.** When Taft learned this, he decided to run. He thought Bryan's ideas about how to run the government were **radical.** He believed that if Bryan were president, he might ruin the country.

Taft leaned heavily on Roosevelt to gain support as he ran for office. Nellie grew irritated because he constantly mentioned Roosevelt's name in his **campaign** speeches. She wanted her husband to appear confident and independent. But Taft felt more confident with Roosevelt behind him.

Taft was the first president to receive a salary of $75,000 per year. Before Taft, the president's salary had been $50,000.

Taft and the vice presidential candidate, James Sherman, won the election of 1908. A terrible blizzard blew in on the day of their **inauguration.** Taft joked, "I always said it would be a cold day when I got to be president of the United States." His presidency would soon prove to be even more miserable for Taft.

One of Taft's most basic problems as president was that people wanted him to be like Theodore Roosevelt. Roosevelt and Taft were very different. Roosevelt was good at selling his ideas to Congress and to the public. Taft was a quieter, more private man. As president, he tended to avoid arguments and did not push his ideas.

President Taft expanded the US Postal Service to include parcel post. This meant that in addition to letters, the post office would also deliver packages. Parcel post was important because at the time, most people lived in rural areas away from cities. It was difficult and expensive for them to send and receive goods.

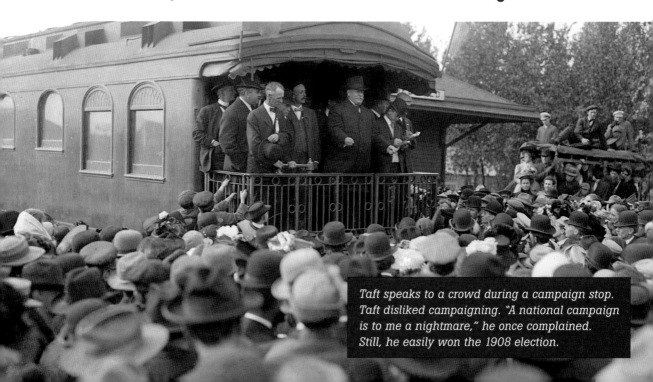

Taft speaks to a crowd during a campaign stop. Taft disliked campaigning. "A national campaign is to me a nightmare," he once complained. Still, he easily won the 1908 election.

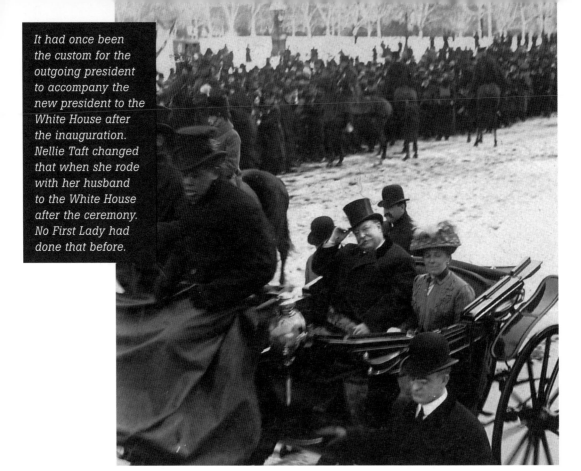

The Tafts were the first presidential family to own automobiles. Taft loved driving— especially driving fast. He said that it helped him relax. President Taft had the White House horse stables remodeled into a garage to house his four cars.

President Taft began his term trying to continue Roosevelt's **progressive** work. The progressive Republicans wanted to improve life for the average citizen. They worked to pass laws that would help small businesses and farmers.

The **conservative** Republicans in Congress were loyal to big businesses. They believed that government should not interfere with business. Two powerful Congressmen, Senator Nelson Aldrich and Representative Joseph Cannon, stopped many **bills** that the progressives tried to pass.

Taft had difficulty working with the conservative Republicans. Unlike Roosevelt, he believed that the president had limited power. He did not think a president should use his power to make Congress pass certain laws. Because he liked to consider issues carefully, Taft also tended to procrastinate, or wait until it was too late to act. This angered some progressives, who felt Taft was not working hard enough to promote their programs. It looked as if Taft's presidency would be a difficult one.

Taft began the presidential tradition of throwing out the first pitch at the start of baseball season. His first throw was at the season opener between the Washington Senators and the Philadelphia Athletics on April 14, 1910.

Theodore Roosevelt (left) and William Taft were once close friends. Their relationship soured during Taft's presidency.

TAFT'S "BATTLE WITH THE BULGE"

William Taft was the heaviest president in American history. The Tafts installed a specially designed bathtub in the White House for him. It was large enough to fit four grown men. They also installed an oversized bathtub in his home in the Philippines. Despite his size, Taft remained agile and athletic. He was considered a good dancer, and he played tennis and golf.

Taft's weight problem was caused by stress. He overate during difficult times and then slimmed down when he was happy. He was at his heaviest close to the end of his presidency. Later, as a professor and Supreme Court justice, he lost weight.

As with other tough problems in his life, Taft tried to keep a sense of humor about his size. While in the Philippines, he sent a message to Secretary of War Elihu Root about his travels. He reported that the trip had gone well, even though he had ridden on horseback high into the mountains for 25 miles (40 km). Root sent a message back asking, "How is the horse?" Rather than being offended, Taft thought the remark was funny and even passed on the story to newspaper reporters.

CHAPTER FOUR

FAILURE AND SUCCESS

Taft never really wanted to be president. Maybe because of this, he is not remembered as a great leader. Still, during his term he worked to make positive changes for the country. Taft passed laws to improve working conditions for railroad and mine workers. He also pushed through a law to reduce the workday for government employees to eight hours a day. Taft appointed Julia Lathrop as head of the children's bureau of the Labor Department. This was the first appointment of a woman as head of a bureau in the **federal** government. During Taft's service as president, two new states joined the Union—New Mexico and Arizona.

President Taft tried to expand US business interests into other parts of the world. He encouraged bankers and businessmen to invest in foreign countries.

Taft was unsure of himself as president. "I feel just a little bit like a fish out of water," he once said.

In 1912, President Taft appointed Julia Lathrop, a social welfare advocate, as head of the US Children's Bureau. While head of the bureau, Lathrop addressed problems in child labor and maternity and infant care, and she worked to improve treatment for people with mental illness.

This became known as "dollar **diplomacy**," because Taft hoped to use money instead of warfare to make the country more powerful overseas.

Taft continued Roosevelt's efforts to break up **trusts.** Trusts were businesses that become so large that they could control the entire **market** for certain products. The trusts drove smaller companies out of business. Since the trust was then the only company making the product it sold, people had no choice but to buy from it.

Taft liked to follow the same routine every day. He played golf in the morning, took a quick nap after lunch, and played bridge after dinner.

The first cross-country airplane flight took place in 1911, during Taft's presidency.

Although Taft had some success as president, he also had many problems. He was a poor politician who had trouble making Congress agree with his ideas. An example was his effort to pass a tariff bill. Tariffs are taxes on goods that are **imported** from other countries. Taft asked Congress to pass a bill that would lower these taxes. US businesses liked high tariffs because it meant more people would be more likely to buy American-made goods since they were less expensive. But the progressives wanted lower tariffs so more Americans could afford imported goods.

The progressives tried hard to pass the bill to lower tariffs. The conservatives tried just as hard to stop it from passing. Although Taft worked to improve the bill, he did not try to convince Congress to pass it.

Congress debated the tariff issue for months. Finally, it passed the Payne-Aldrich tariff bill. This bill was a **compromise.** Neither the conservatives nor the progressives really got what they wanted. The bill cut tariffs on most items but raised tariffs on others.

Taft knew the bill was not exactly what his party wanted, but he thought it improved the situation overall. The newspapers did not see it that way. They attacked Taft as a **traitor** to his party. Still, Taft did not defend himself or the bill.

Taft ran into another sticky problem dealing with land **conservation.** At that time, there were still huge tracts of wild land in the United States. On some of this land, people could homestead, or claim the land as theirs simply by settling on it. The government kept land if it had natural **resources,** such as minerals or oil. President Roosevelt had also set aside large amounts of land that did not have resources. This land would become national parks and forests.

Nellie Taft had gardeners plant the 3,000 cherry trees that still adorn the White House lawn. The trees were a gift from the Japanese ambassador. Mrs. Taft personally planted the first two saplings with the Japanese ambassador's wife.

Taft and his family had long spent summers at Murray Bay in Canada. After he became president, however, Taft felt he should spend summers in his own country. The Tafts found a cottage in Massachusetts, where they escaped Washington's summer heat. It became known as the Summer White House.

As the head of the US Forest Service, Gifford Pinchot greatly increased the size and number of national forests in the United States. He promoted the idea that forests should be preserved for the future.

When Taft became president, his **secretary of the interior,** Richard A. Ballinger, was careful about what land he claimed for the government. He only set aside lands that were proven to have valuable resources. This angered Gifford Pinchot, the head of the US Forest Service. It also upset a man named Louis R. Glavis, who worked with Ballinger at the Department of the Interior. Pinchot and Glavis wanted to keep more land for the government, especially for parks and forests.

Glavis accused Ballinger of helping oil companies take land away from the government. Taft stepped in to solve the argument. In his judgelike manner, he looked at evidence and listened to both sides.

In the end, he found that Ballinger had done nothing wrong. In fact, Glavis had been dishonest, and he was fired.

Glavis was angry and spoke to reporters, who ran the story without checking to see if the facts were correct. Pinchot continued to support Glavis. At this point, Taft had no choice but to fire Pinchot. Roosevelt had appointed Pinchot initially. Firing him made Taft look as if he were turning against the progressives and against Roosevelt.

The *Titanic* sank in 1912, during Taft's presidency. More than 1,500 people died.

When people criticized him, Taft apologized for being president, assuring them that there would soon be someone better in the White House.

Taft was the first president to play golf as a hobby. He enjoyed the game's slow pace and the time he spent on the course with his friends.

Taft began to lose the support of many progressive Republicans. Without them, he had to turn to the conservative Republicans for advice and help. This angered the progressives even more.

In 1910, Theodore Roosevelt returned from a lengthy trip to Africa. He discovered that the Republican Party was a mess. He made statements indicating that he thought Taft was doing a bad job as president. This wounded Taft. "I am deeply hurt," he said. "And it is hard, very hard . . . to see a devoted friendship going to pieces."

Theodore Roosevelt (center) competed with Taft for the presidency in 1912. The two men had once been friends, but they became bitter rivals.

Taft shakes hands with newly elected President Wilson on the day of Wilson's inauguration. Taft was glad to be leaving the White House. "Politics makes me sick," he once complained.

By the next presidential election in 1912, Taft had lost Roosevelt's backing. He and Roosevelt were no longer friends. The stress from these problems caused Taft to overeat. Near the end of his term as president, Taft's weight reached 355 pounds (161 kg).

As president, Taft still had enough support to be nominated as the Republican Party candidate in 1912. Roosevelt started his own **political party** to run against Taft. He called it the Progressive Party, but it was also known as the Bull Moose Party. Splitting the Republican Party also split the Republican vote. This allowed the Democratic candidate, Woodrow Wilson, to easily win the election. Roosevelt and Taft never renewed their friendship.

Leaving the White House after losing the election of 1912 did not make Taft sad. "I'm glad to be going," he told the new president, Woodrow Wilson. "This is the lonesomest place in the world." Nellie Taft was miserable, however. While her husband lunched with the Wilsons, she stayed upstairs packing her bags.

WOMEN FIGHT
FOR RIGHTS

Women have long struggled to have the same rights as men. For much of the United States' history, women did not have the right to vote.

In the past, most women did not work outside the home or become involved in politics. Some women didn't like this lack of freedom. Beginning in 1866, a group of women banned together to change this situation. They believed women should have rights equal to men. They wanted to be able to vote and work in all types of jobs. Women across the country began to form groups to rally for their rights, particularly the right to vote. They wanted Congress to pass an **amendment** to allow women across the country the right to vote. This was called the **suffrage** movement.

During the 1900s, more women became active in politics and the workplace. In the 1912 presidential election, women worked actively for both parties. They made speeches and held rallies in support of their candidate. Yet by this time, there was still no national law giving women the right to vote.

Taft understood that women wanted better lives. He believed in better working conditions for women. But he was against suffrage. First Lady Nellie Taft (below) disagreed. She even became a member of a suffrage club. She called herself a "qualified" suffragist. This meant she thought both men and women should vote if they could prove they understood the issues.

Taft's Democratic opponent in the 1912 election, Woodrow Wilson, was also against women's suffrage. Of the three candidates in that election, only Theodore Roosevelt supported it. Many women supported Roosevelt, but Wilson won the presidency.

Women continued fighting for the right to vote. Finally, in 1919, Congress passed the 19th amendment to the Constitution, which extended the vote to women. The next year, the amendment went into effect, and women voted in an American presidential election for the first time.

Instead of being disappointed by his defeat, Taft was relieved. He was happy to leave politics. He became a professor of law at Yale University, and he spent the next eight years teaching, writing books, and lecturing. He wrote a book about the presidency called *Our Chief Magistrate and His Powers* that is still a respected work.

In 1921, Taft fulfilled a lifelong dream when President Warren Harding appointed him chief justice of the United States Supreme Court.

Taft is remembered as one of the most effective chief justices in US history. He moved cases quickly through the Court and worked tirelessly every day. He even convinced the government to pay for a beautiful new building for the Supreme Court.

Chief Justice Taft, extremely happy on the job, dropped a good deal of weight. He held the position of chief justice for more than eight years. Taft's success on the Supreme Court erased the unhappiness he felt as president. "I don't remember that I ever was president," he wrote shortly before his death.

Taft had suffered from digestive problems and small heart attacks for years. He did not want to retire, even though he was ill. Taft finally left his position on the Supreme Court only a month before his death. He died on March 8, 1930, in Washington, DC. He was 72 years old.

William Taft was buried at Arlington National Cemetery in Virginia. His wife, Nellie, lived for 13 years after her husband's death. She traveled and watched her children carry on the Taft tradition of education and the law. She died on May 22, 1943, at the age of 81.

Taft was the first president to be buried at Arlington National Cemetery, a burial ground for the nation's heroes. John F. Kennedy is the only other president buried there.

The Cincinnati home where William Howard Taft was born and raised is now a national historic site.

TIME LINE

1857
William Taft is born to Alphonso and Louisa Taft in Cincinnati, Ohio, on September 15.

1878
William Taft graduates from Yale University.

1879
Taft meets Helen "Nellie" Herron, whom he will later marry.

1880
Taft graduates from Cincinnati Law School and becomes licensed to practice law.

1882
President Chester Arthur appoints Taft tax collector for the Cincinnati area.

1886
Taft marries Helen "Nellie" Herron on June 19.

1887
Taft is appointed to the Ohio Superior Court.

1890
President Benjamin Harrison appoints Taft US solicitor general.

1892
Taft becomes a judge on the US Circuit Court.

1900
Taft is appointed president of the US commission to establish order in the Philippines. He and his family travel to Manila, where they will live for the next four years.

1901
Taft becomes governor of the Philippines. During his term, he helps construct roads, organize local governments, and set up schools, courts, and basic services for the people. In September, Taft is offered a position on the Supreme Court, but he decides to stay in the Philippines.

1904
President Theodore Roosevelt appoints Taft secretary of war. The two men become friends.

1908
Roosevelt encourages Taft to run for president. Taft is reluctant but agrees. With Roosevelt's backing, Taft wins the Republican Party's nomination for president and then the election.

1909
Taft is inaugurated the 27th president of the United States. He urges Congress to reduce tariffs, and a battle among progressives and conservatives begins.

1910
Taft and Roosevelt have a falling out after Taft fires Gifford Pinchot, the head of the US Forest Service and an ally of Roosevelt's.

1912
Taft appoints Julia Lathrop the head of the children's bureau of the Department of Labor, making her the first woman to head a bureau in the federal government. New Mexico and Arizona are admitted to the Union. Roosevelt starts his own political party to run against Taft for the presidency. Both Taft and Roosevelt lose the election to Democrat Woodrow Wilson.

1913
Taft becomes a professor of constitutional law at Yale University.

1921
Taft is appointed chief justice of the US Supreme Court.

1930
Taft retires from the Supreme Court on February 3. On March 8, he dies at age 72.

1943
On May 22, Helen "Nellie" Herron Taft dies at age 81.

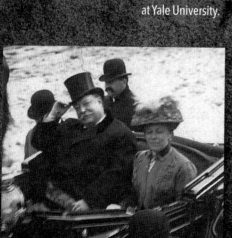

amendment (uh-MEND-munt): An amendment is a change or addition made to the US Constitution or other document. The 19th Amendment gave American women the right to vote.

appointed (uh-POYN-ted): If someone is appointed to a position, he or she is asked by an important official to accept the position. President Harding appointed Taft the chief justice of the Supreme Court.

bills (BILZ): Bills are proposed new laws. Congress must pass a bill and the president must sign it before a bill becomes a law.

cabinet (KAB-nit): The cabinet is the group of people who advise a president. As the secretary of war, Taft was a member of President Roosevelt's cabinet.

campaign (kam-PAYN): A campaign is the process of running for an election, including activities such as giving speeches or attending rallies. Taft said a presidential campaign was a nightmare.

candidate (KAN-duh-dayt): A candidate is a person who is running in an election. At least two candidates run for president every four years.

commission (kuh-MISH-un): A commission is a group of people appointed to do something. Taft served as president of the commission sent to establish US control in the Philippines.

compromise (KOM-pruh-myz): A compromise is a way to settle a disagreement in which both sides give up part of what they want.

conservation (kon-ser-VAY-shun): Conservation is the practice of protecting something from being lost or used up. The progressive Republicans believed in land conservation.

conservative (kun-SER-vuh-tiv): In politics, a conservative is someone who wants to make few changes in the government. President Taft began to meet with conservative Republicans when he lost support from progressive Republicans.

diplomacy (dih-PLOH-muh-see): Diplomacy is when a government uses careful actions to make sure it gets along with other nations. Taft used "dollar diplomacy" to improve relations with other countries.

federal (FED-ur-ul): Federal means having to do with the central government of the United States, rather than a state or city government. Taft was the first president to appoint a woman to an important federal government position.

imported (im-POR-ted): If a product is imported, it has been brought in from a foreign country for sale or use. Tariffs on imported goods made them more expensive to buy than American goods.

inauguration (ih-naw-gyuh-RAY-shun): An inauguration is the ceremony that takes place when a new president begins a term of office. The weather was bad on Taft's inauguration day.

labor unions (LAY-bur YOON-yenz): Labor unions are groups of workers who join together to try to improve working conditions. Labor unions and businesses often disagreed during the late 1800s.

market (MAR-kit): A market is the buying and selling of a specific product. Some companies controlled a market for a certain product by owning many smaller businesses that made the same product.

nomination (nom-uh-NAY-shun): If someone receives a nomination, he or she is chosen by a political party to run for an office. Taft won the presidential nomination of the Republican Party in 1908.

political party (puh-LIT-uh-kul PAR-tee): A political party is a group of people who share similar ideas about how to run a government. The two major US political parties are the Democrats and the Republicans.

politics (PAWL-uh-tiks): Politics refers to the actions and practices of the government. Taft preferred to work in law rather than in politics.

prejudice (PRE-ju-dus): Prejudice is an unreasonable hatred or fear of others. Taft tried to find jobs for African Americans in the government, but it was difficult because prejudice against them was so strong.

progressive (pruh-GRESS-iv): A progressive is a person who believes the government should work to improve society. Taft and Roosevelt believed in progressive ideas.

prosecutor (PRAH-seh-kyoo-tur): A prosecutor is a lawyer who works for the government. Taft was appointed assistant prosecutor of Hamilton County.

radical (RAD-uh-kul): If an idea is radical, it is very different from the way things are usually done. William Jennings Bryan had radical ideas about government.

resources (REE-sor-sez): Resources are things that can be used to benefit people, such as oil or water. The government often controls land with valuable natural resources.

revolution (rev-uh-LOO-shun): A revolution is a complete change in government. Rebels led a revolution in Cuba.

salary (SAL-ree): A salary is money a person is paid regularly for work. As president, Taft received a salary of $75,000 a year.

secretary of the interior (SEK-ruh-tayr-ee OF THE in-TEER-ee-ur): The secretary of the interior is a member of the president's cabinet. He or she heads the department in charge of how US land is used.

solicitor (suh-LIS-uh-tur): A solicitor is another word for a lawyer. President Harrison named Taft the solicitor general.

strike (STRYK): If workers go on strike, they refuse to do their jobs until their employers agree to something. Workers might strike to demand better pay or shorter hours.

suffrage (SUF-rij): Suffrage is the right to vote. Women worked for suffrage during Taft's 1912 presidential campaign.

traitor (TRAY-ter): A traitor is a person who betrays his or her country. Some people said Taft was a traitor to his party.

treaty (TREE-tee): A treaty is a formal agreement between nations. In the treaty that ended the Spanish-American War, Spain gave the United States control of the Philippines.

trusts (TRUSTS): Trusts are large businesses that control the entire market for certain products. Presidents Taft and Roosevelt tried to break up trusts.

THE UNITED STATES GOVERNMENT

The United States government is divided into three equal branches: the executive, the legislative, and the judicial. This division helps prevent abuses of power because each branch has to answer to the other two. No one branch can become too powerful.

EXECUTIVE BRANCH

President
Vice President
Departments

The job of the executive branch is to enforce the laws. It is headed by the president, who serves as the spokesperson for the United States around the world. The president has the power to sign bills into law. He or she also appoints important officials, such as federal judges, who are then confirmed by the US Senate. The president is also the commander in chief of the US military. He or she is assisted by the vice president, who takes over if the president dies or cannot carry out the duties of the office.

The executive branch also includes various departments, each focused on a specific topic. They include the Defense Department, the Justice Department, and the Agriculture Department. The department heads, along with other officials such as the vice president, serve as the president's closest advisers, called the cabinet.

LEGISLATIVE BRANCH

Congress: Senate and the
House of Representatives

The job of the legislative branch is to make the laws. It consists of Congress, which is divided into two parts: the Senate and the House of Representatives. The Senate has 100 members, and the House of Representatives has 435 members. Each state has two senators. The number of representatives a state has varies depending on the state's population.

Besides making laws, Congress also passes budgets and enacts taxes. In addition, it is responsible for declaring war, maintaining the military, and regulating trade with other countries.

JUDICIAL BRANCH

Supreme Court
Courts of Appeals
District Courts

The job of the judicial branch is to interpret the laws. It consists of the nation's federal courts. Trials are held in district courts. During trials, judges must decide what laws mean and how they apply. Courts of appeals review the decisions made in district courts.

The nation's highest court is the Supreme Court. If someone disagrees with a court of appeals ruling, he or she can ask the Supreme Court to review it. The Supreme Court may refuse. The Supreme Court makes sure that decisions and laws do not violate the Constitution.

CHOOSING THE PRESIDENT

It may seem odd, but American voters don't elect the president directly. Instead, the president is chosen using what is called the Electoral College.

Each state gets as many votes in the Electoral College as its combined total of senators and representatives in Congress. For example, Iowa has two senators and four representatives, so it gets six electoral votes. Although the District of Columbia does not have any voting members in Congress, it gets three electoral votes. Usually, the candidate who wins the most votes in any given state receives all of that state's electoral votes.

To become president, a candidate must get more than half of the Electoral College votes. There are a total of 538 votes in the Electoral College, so a candidate needs 270 votes to win. If nobody receives 270 Electoral College votes, the House of Representatives chooses the president.

With the Electoral College system, the person who receives the most votes nationwide does not always receive the most electoral votes. This happened most recently in 2016, when Hillary Clinton received nearly 2.9 million more national votes than Donald J. Trump. Trump became president because he had more Electoral College votes.

The White House is the official home of the president of the United States. It is located at 1600 Pennsylvania Avenue NW in Washington, DC. In 1792, a contest was held to select the architect who would design the president's home. James Hoban won. Construction took eight years.

The first president, George Washington, never lived in the White House. The second president, John Adams, moved into the house in 1800, though the inside was not yet complete. During the War of 1812, British soldiers burned down much of the White House. It was rebuilt several years later.

The White House was changed through the years. Porches were added, and President Theodore Roosevelt added the West Wing. President William Taft changed the shape of the presidential office, making it into the famous Oval Office. While Harry Truman was president, the old house was discovered to be structurally weak. All the walls were reinforced with steel, and the rooms were rebuilt.

Today, the White House has 132 rooms (including 35 bathrooms), 28 fireplaces, and 3 elevators. It takes 570 gallons of paint to cover the outside of the six-story building. The White House provides the president with many ways to relax. It includes a putting green, a jogging track, a swimming pool, a basketball and tennis court, and beautifully landscaped gardens. The White House also has a movie theater, a billiard room, and a one-lane bowling alley.

PRESIDENTIAL PERKS

The job of president of the United States is challenging. It is probably one of the most stressful jobs in the world. Because of this, presidents are paid well, though not nearly as well as the leaders of large corporations. In 2020, the president earned $400,000 a year. Presidents also receive extra benefits that make the demanding job a little more appealing.

★ **Camp David:** In the 1940s, President Franklin D. Roosevelt chose this heavily wooded spot in the mountains of Maryland to be the presidential retreat, where presidents can relax. Even though it is a retreat, world business is conducted there. Most famously, President Jimmy Carter met with Middle Eastern leaders at Camp David in 1978. The result was a peace agreement between Israel and Egypt.

★ *Air Force One:* The president flies on a jet called *Air Force One*. It is a Boeing 747-200B that has been modified to meet the president's needs. *Air Force One* is the size of a large home. It is equipped with a dining room, sleeping quarters, a conference room, and office space. It also has two kitchens that can provide food for up to 100 people.

★ **The Secret Service:** While not the most glamorous of the president's perks, the Secret Service is one of the most important. The Secret Service is a group of highly trained agents who protect the president and the president's family.

★ **The Presidential State Car:** The presidential state car is a customized Cadillac limousine. It has been armored to protect the president in case of attack. Inside the plush car are a foldaway desk, an entertainment center, and a communications console.

★ **The Food:** The White House has five chefs who will make any food the president wants. The White House also has an extensive wine collection and vegetable and fruit gardens.

★ **Retirement:** A former president receives a pension, or retirement pay, of just under $208,000 a year. Former presidents also receive health care coverage and Secret Service protection for the rest of their lives.

QUALIFICATIONS

To run for president, a candidate must

- ★ be at least 35 years old
- ★ be a citizen who was born in the United States
- ★ have lived in the United States for 14 years

TERM OF OFFICE

A president's term of office is four years. No president can stay in office for more than two terms.

ELECTION DATE

The presidential election takes place every four years on the first Tuesday after November 1.

INAUGURATION DATE

Presidents are inaugurated on January 20.

OATH OF OFFICE

I do solemnly swear I will faithfully execute the office of the President of the United States and will to the best of my ability preserve, protect, and defend the Constitution of the United States.

WRITE A LETTER TO THE PRESIDENT

One of the best things about being a US citizen is that Americans get to participate in their government. They can speak out if they feel government leaders aren't doing their jobs. They can also praise leaders who are going the extra mile. Do you have something you'd like the president to do? Should the president worry more about the environment and the effects of climate change? Should the government spend more money on our schools? You can write a letter to the president to say how you feel!

> 1600 Pennsylvania Avenue NW
> Washington, DC 20500

You can even write a message to the president at **whitehouse.gov/contact**.

FOR MORE INFORMATION

BOOKS

Roesser, Marie. *The Panama Canal.*
New York, NY: Gareth Stevens, 2020.

Sonneborn, Liz. *The Supreme Court: Why It Matters to You.*
New York, NY: Children's Press, 2019.

Sullivan, George. *Scholastic Book of Presidents.*
New York, NY: Scholastic, 2020.

Vink, Amanda. *Suffragists and Those Who Opposed Them.*
New York, NY: PowerKids, 2019.

Wassner Flynn, Sarah. *1,000 Facts about the White House.*
Washington, DC: National Geographic Kids, 2017.

INTERNET SITES

Visit our website for lots of links about
William Howard Taft and other US presidents:

childsworld.com/links

Note to Parents, Teachers, and Librarians: We routinely verify our web links to make sure they are safe, active sites. Encourage your readers to check them out!

INDEX